FINDING THE LEADER WITHIN

16 Ways Women in Leadership Can Balance Work and Home

Dedication

This book is dedicated to my grandmother, Emo and my daughters Uneeka and Kayla. My granddaughter London. I love you so much, it stinks.

Table Of Contents

Acknowledgements

To my grandmother Emo, thank you for all the prayers, introducing me to the daily word and not giving up on me. You have helped me develop into the woman I am today.

To my daughters, Uneeka and Kayla, and my grandaughter London you are my why. Thank you for believing in me when I didn't believe in myself.

To my aunts and uncles, I owe you big time. When my mother died you didn't hesitate to step up and help raise me. I love you from the bottom of my heart.

To my sister Sharoya, thank you for being you. I love you.

To Corey, thank you for being my right hand.

To all the professional women, thank you for being the leader of your life, your career, business and your family. I pray the words in this book encourage you to keep going even though life can get tough at times. You're doing a fantastic job. Keep up the good work.

Foreword

*B*eing a leader means being able to take control over your life. All my life, my mom has been making me sit in the mirror and repeat affirmations while doing my day to day routine. She said these things would improve my day to day life and make it more peaceful, happy, and better. The activities, the affirmations, and the motivational talks were seeds she was planting so I can reach the top. Whatever situation you are in, *Finding the Leader Within* will help you get through and get over obstacles. We are trying to jump over all these obstacles that they put in the field of life and surpass to the finish line (success). Success can be for us to have peace of mind, to be happy, to be a better mom, or to be a better person. Some of us love to take shortcuts in life. We tend to think that going to church isn't a necessity, or planning out our day isn't important, or just going through life day to day is how living is.

Let me bring you back to 3rd grade for a minute. Do you remember the story of the tortoise and the hare? For those who don't know the story, *The Tortoise and the Hare* is one of Aesop's Fables. The story is about of a race between unequal partners. It is itself a variant of a common folktale theme in which ingenuity and trickery are employed to overcome a stronger opponent. The tortoise and hare are set out for a race and everyone knows that a tortoise is extremely slow and a hare is very fast. Every animal knew that the hare would win because he was so fast. When the race started, the hare set off, taking shortcuts. He took naps while the tortoise moved on slowly and didn't take any short cuts through the forest. With so much confidence, the tortoise still went on. Can you guess who won? Most, maybe all, would say the hare, although it was the tortoise.

The hare fell asleep and forgot about the race thinking that he had so much time. The moral comparison I'm trying to make is in life you can't take shortcuts or worry about what the other person is doing. You have to set a goal and stick through that goal no matter how slow you are or how many obstacles are in your way. In this book, *Finding the Leader Within*, you can learn to become that tortoise. We all go through things in life, whether it's not being able to make time for the important things in life, or that we are in debt, or that we are having problems in our relationships. *Finding the Leader Within* helps you put these problems in the back seat. Like I said, you will adapt the book to your lifestyle in the way that you need it to fix your life, but the book is a diverse way to help with all problems.

We all have multiple responsibilities in life, and they can become overwhelming. Sometimes we let these responsibilities take over our ability to take care of ourselves. We have to keep that light on in our heads so we do not lose sight of the leader that lies within us. Being the leader of your life is important because if you don't lead yourself, someone else will. Run your own race and keep reading.

Uneeka Powell

Introduction

A few years ago, my life went down a dark alley. It was in shambles and collapsing before my eyes. This was caused mainly by the toxic relationship which I had kept both with myself and with my partner. Looking back at the story of how it all started, I realize now, how much a moment's decision can change everything.

It all started with a casual stroll! I remember how my partner walked up to me and asked me for my number. I politely declined at first and walked away; but he was a persistent man. He came around to ask again.

When next we came across each other, he asked again, and it was then that I made what would turn out to be my greatest mistake! I thought to myself, "What do I have to lose?" Fate would later provide the answer to this question, and it was in no nice way! I had everything to lose. This would be the beginning of what would later prove to be a very toxic relationship that caused a decline in almost all aspects of my life; I saw decreases in my faith, family, finances, health and education. I fell into huge debts, borrowing from Peter to pay Paul. I went from the 700 club straight down to the 400s. I was neglecting my health, family, faith, and finances. I was a complete mess and my life was in shambles. I would miss important appointments and my education got the worst hit.

I was in nursing school and was supposed to be studying for my examinations; yet I couldn't stay focused due to the toll my relationship was taking on my life. I was being abused, physically and mentally. It was so terrible that one day, after a heated argument, which by the way had become a regular occurrence, I found myself on the floor, weeping my eyes out; yet my partner stood over me and was laughing to his heart's content. The contrast and irony crushed what was left of my spirit. It battered what was left of my esteem and broke me in tiny pieces. However, in the midst of my darkness, was ushered unto me a streak of life that would go on to lead to my salvation. For it was that particular ugly scenario that got me to reassess my station in life. I thought to myself that enough was enough. I couldn't continue like that; I had to get my life back. I had to take charge and be the leader of my life once more. I was done having someone lead me to my own destruction.

I took out time to engage in some self-reflection. I needed to know why I was at this point in my life. How come I could provide solutions to other people's problems, yet couldn't fix my own? I had to evaluate the niche I was occupying in the universe and the signal I was giving out by my thoughts, words, actions, and life. I thought to myself that it was time to do some house cleaning, to remove the clutters of negativity that were hindering my access to greater glory. This exercise taught me the importance of self-reflection. Conscious effort is required to change a negative story. This is because, as I noticed, negativity is easier to take roots; it takes 13 positive things to get rid of one negative thing. What is more, the more negative your thinking, the more it is that you engineer your reality to replicate the negative thoughts. The law of attraction is a potent force, and it brings to each one what they envision and solicit with their thinking.

It is from the vast lessons learned and in the confidence gained from life's stings that I put out this book to serve as a guide to everybody who is walking a similar path that is my past. I also want to provide illumination to others that they may not walk this route. This book is intended to be a lamp to your feet on how to rebuild your foundation to make it sturdier, stronger, and resilient. It is a book to keep you focused, letting no one distract you on your path to self-realization. It is one to help you rebuild your faith, family, finances, health and education in cases where there have been cracks.

Setting Your Leadership Standard

CHAPTER 1:

Prioritizing God

> *"The secret of a happy life is giving God the first part of your day, the first priority in every decision, and the first place in your heart,"* Joi U Grant

It is important to give God the first part of your day. I remember while growing up, I was taught to read the *Daily Word* on a daily basis. In those days, it was unclear to me why my grandmother was bent on causing me so much *pain,* at least in my opinion, by making me read it every morning. To run away from my pain, I used to try to sneak out of the house every morning, but my grandma always had a way of knowing when my hands touched the door knob. I have never been able to understand how she was able to do that. My young mind was unable to recognize that she was planting seeds into my life; I had no way of grasping the far-reaching blessings brought by this painful exercise. It was only in later years that it all began to come home to me. I found joy in being with the Lord. Yet, in those days, I greatly dreaded what she made me go through. I remember a particular time when I was reading a passage aloud with tears streaming down my eyes and snot running down my nose. In hindsight, I must admit that those years were the happiest days of my life; it was a time when I had more focus.

It took the fog that enveloped my life during my 20's, when I finally broke away from the presence of God, for me to realize what golden moments those days had been. My 20's were marked by a loss of direction, and I was walking around in a daze.

It got worse into my early 30's as I stopped reading the scriptures entirely and stopped going to church. I was embroiled in a maze and acted on the promptings of a world that sucked me in and weakened my spirit. I tried to remain focused, but I just couldn't. I was trying to be the director of my own life, and the fact that I was doing a poor job of it was obvious.

It wasn't long before I walked into a toxic relationship. As he approached me, trying to talk to me, I remember thinking: *Keep walking. It's not worth it.* Yet, at the same time, there was another voice asking: *what do you have to lose? You must follow your gut.* I had a lot to lose, as it turned out. I had everything from my faith, to my family, my finances, my health, and education to lose. I was losing the foundation of my faith; everything I believed in was being taken away from me. I was studying but barely passing or not passing at all. I was in nursing school at the time and was scheduled to take a promotional exam. I failed the nursing exam and did not show up for the promotional exam.

It was then I realized I was trying to lead my life myself, with all my human failings, and the result was not going so well. I realized I had to return to where it all started to rediscover the reason why things worked out so well in the past and why things had stopped working for me. It then occurred to me that I needed to put my trust and faith in God and let him lead my life again. The moment I made this decision, everything began to fall into place again. He made all my crooked lines straight.

Making this decision wasn't easy at first. I didn't know where to start. I recall calling the *Unity Prayer Line* and speaking to a lady on the other end. She was helpful; I explained what was going on with me. She referred me to the scriptures that pertained to what I was going through. She then asked me a question, which struck me greatly; she wanted to know what my prayer routine was like. I told her I didn't have a prayer routine. She understood and then began explaining the priceless truth, which I have found to hold steadfast ever since. She said, "Okay, when you seek God first in your daily pursuits, He promises to add unto you those things which you are pursuing as long as they are in His will. "Oh sugar! I got it," I said. Then, I started reading Psalms 91. I read it daily to rediscover the goodness of the promises which He has made to those who walk with Him.

I made a morning prayer routine. This wasn't an easy task at all. I set aside time in the morning to talk with God. It was during this time that I noticed that as you increase your faith, obstacles and distractions will come in many folds. However, when they do, don't stop. You are on the right track.

It was then that I started reading the *Daily Word* again, like I did in my childhood days. I also read the Bible for 5 minutes and prayed for five more. I sat still and meditated to listen to what God had to say. I then increased the time I spent with Him to 10 minutes. The result was instant and glaring as my life changed. I started praying before I did anything and before making any decision. As a result, the abundant blessings of God have been added unto my life, bringing no sorrow as He indeed promises all those who walk in His light!

Reflection

- Are you putting God first in your life?

- What are some things that you are going through in your life that have defied you? Maybe it's time you turned it over to God.

- What is your daily prayer routine?

- Are you living your life from the point of your own abilities? It's time to seek out the overwhelming powers of God. Do this and see the difference.

CHAPTER 2:

———◆———

Forgiveness

> *The feeling I felt thereafter gave me the courage and strength to move forward," ~Joi U. Grant*

*F*orgiveness does not change the past wrong done to you. As a matter of fact, the damage done by the wrong may persist for a long time if it's not entirely irremediable. It is for this that forgiveness may prove a hard and difficult thing to do. However, failing to forgive those who have wronged you may act to block you from receiving God's blessings and forgiveness as well. We are judged by whatever standard we use in measuring others. This being said, we know that forgiveness can sometimes prove difficult.

The following are some suggested steps to achieving forgiveness for others:

☐ **Step 1: Tell them exactly how you feel**

The first step to forgiveness involves letting out the bottled up feelings of anger in your heart. I recall a time I felt so badly about a person. I just grabbed him and told him exactly how I felt about his attitude towards me. I felt lighter inside. Sometimes, the people that have wronged us might not even know this. Hence, they don't apologize until you bring it to their attention. An apology, if it comes, brings a sense of closure to you. However, if it doesn't come, forgive for your own need and for God's forgiveness.

☐ **Step 2:** Always remember that God loves you so much and there are a lot of others who love and respect you. So, make sure that your self-worth doesn't rest on a person's negative response to you.

☐ **Step 3:** Ask for extra strength to forgive as well as for the grace to trust again.

☐ **Step 4:** Make a decision to forgive as an act for your well-being, both psychological and spiritual.

☐ **Step 5:** Discuss the issue with your friends and family as the pains may be eased by the soothing words from another person.

I recall a time in my life when I was just seven years old and my twenty-seven-year-old mother had just died. I had no one to explain the situation, and I was so angry. I actually didn't understand what was going on and why she died at such a young age. I was angry with her for leaving me alone so soon before I could have a relationship with her. My bitterness affected me deeply and dictated my relationship with others. Later on, when I saw myself in a toxic relationship and kept on making the same mistakes in my relationship, I had to take out time for some self-reflection. It was only then that I was able to take a journey down memory lane to the time when it all started, the time when I was just seven. It was then I realized that I was still upset with my mother. I had not forgiven her for leaving me. I realized that I needed to take the time out and learn forgiveness. It wasn't so much for any other person, but it was for me. If I wanted to move on, then it was time to drop the heavy yolk; I had to move away from the thing that was holding me back from living the way I wanted to live.

To move on, I sat down and actually penned a letter to my mom, explaining how I felt and how I missed her. I went down to the cemetery and read the letter aloud while sitting at her tombstone. At the end, I didn't feel so hurt. In fact, I felt a sense of relief and was able to move forward in my life. The feeling I felt thereafter gave me the courage and the strength to move forward. I have since forgiven her as well as myself.

Until that time, I did not realize that not forgiving my mother and myself had broken me down physically and mentally. It had stopped me from making progress and becoming the woman I am today. It also made me realize that sometimes, when we go through hurt and pain in our hearts and in our subconscious minds, we don't realize that it is a result of our bad attitude towards a situation or experience we had in the past. If you wish to live a life of peace and happiness, you must learn to forgive. This is the only way to be free, happy, and at peace.

When we forget that we are not doing it for the other person but for ourselves, we tend to hold off on forgiveness and live with the anger. We eventually lash out at others who are not in any way involved in the thing we are passing through. In the end, we simply drive people from our lives and become isolated.

This can lead to depression and suicide. Thus, to present a better package and life for ourselves, we must strive to block out all negative feelings. This will enable us to feel lighter, flourish, and sprint through life joyously!

CHAPTER 3:

Living A Purpose Driven Life

> *"The greatest tragedy in life is not death but*
> *life without a purpose"*
> Rick Warren

The next step to finding the leader in you, is finding your purpose. First off, one needs to understand the meaning of purpose.

What Is Purpose?

Purpose can be defined as the aim, vision, goal or dream someone strives for or for which he exists. It is a determined influence and impact we yearn to achieve in life. Ingrained into all our activities, is the purpose of doing them.

Dr Myles Munroe said, "The greatest tragedy in life is not death but life without a purpose." Many people live capriciously, without a purpose. They are gravitating towards a dead end, having no grip on their purpose. They keep running from pillar to post with no purpose in mind. Your happiest day will not be the day you get that multi-million dollar contract, or the day you get married, but it will be the day you discover your purpose of living.

Rick Warren puts it this way:

> *Without clear purpose, you have no foundation upon which to base decision, allocate your time, and use your resources. Without purpose, you tend to make choices based upon circumstances, pressure and your mood at that moment.*

I've come to discover that three sets of people exist in relation to how you make your choices or decisions.

First, there are those that don't make any choice or decision by themselves they need the approval of others. I'm referring to adults here. Adults are products of external influences and choices. Second, there are those whose choices are informed or stimulated by present circumstances. They decide based on their present conditions rather than on their inner convictions. They fail to heed the advice of T.D. Jakes, a well-known evangelist, when he advised, "Don't make permanent decisions based on temporary situations." Finally, there are those whose choices flow from the understanding of their purpose in life. All of your decisions ought to be founded on your purpose in life. Some people spend their entire life looking for their purpose. The reason why we don't find our true purpose is because we look at ourselves first. When we focus on ourselves we will never find our life's purpose. I believe that God has put us here for a reason. You were put here on this earth to do more than go to work, come home, cook dinner, do homework with the kids, watch the t.v and get up to do the same thing over again. Some people feel that this activity is due to productivity. You can be very busy without being effective. You can be active without being productive. Life does not reward busyness, it rewards effectiveness. Managing your time effectively is contingent upon your understanding of your purpose in life. Wasted time results in wasted lives. We spend more time watching Love and Hip Hop and Basketball Wives than we spend finding our true purpose. God designed you to make a difference with your life.

Why Your Purpose Is Important?

Knowing your purpose gives meaning to your life. When your life has meaning, you can handle anything. Without God your life has no meaning. Without meaning, life has no significance. You were made to have meaning.

My advice is to do a self reflection on your life. We all have gifts and talents. You should get a piece of paper and write down what things are you good at doing. What makes you happy? What drives your life? Ask your friends their candid opinion. Your gifts and talents are always confirmed by others.

You have several gifts and abilities you don't know you have because you never tried them out. So I encourage you to try doing things that you never tried before. It might feel uncomfortable at first but remember nothing grows when you're comfortable. No matter how old you are, it's never too late to learn a new skill, finish something you started or go back to school.

Chapter 4:

Your Self Worth Determines Your Net Worth

> *"Being at peace with who you are and what you have to offer the world is a major part of having a high self esteem,"*
> ~Joi U Grant

*H*onestly, seeing ourselves for who we really are is humbling and painful. Typically, women like to avoid pain. As pain is in the driver's seat, fear can be the backseat passenger. Realizing that beyond fear and pain lies freedom, possibility, and healing is the first step in the right direction. We have positives , negatives, and everything in between. Self-awareness requires seeing the truth for what it is. In some cases, the truth hurts.

We as women fight the ongoing battle and struggle between being the person we wish to be vs the person we really are. Self-awareness forces us to accept *"what is* rather than *what should be.* Therefore, it has the potential to cause upset flings. Within ourselves lie strengths and abilities not yet tapped into, ones we may not even be aware of! Self-awareness helps draw out the natural strengths one possesses, and brings them to light. Thus, it is our responsibility to become self-aware so we can further use what we have to help others and fulfill our purpose. From this practice, we can also solve our own problems in a more effective way. So, the practice of self-awareness is necessary in every way.

Why aren't we more aware about ourselves? Distractions. Our fast paced way of living doesn't always allow for us to stop and think to reflect on life. As a result, people forget and/or choose not to take the time needed to check in with themselves, and learn more about themselves.

I once knew this woman who was smart and beautiful. Her smile would light up a room. She had all the latest fashion. Women her age looked up to her. She had her daughter at seventeen and decided to get her GED because she couldn't see herself returning to high school after having a baby. She withdrew from high school and signed up to take the exam. When she was done taking the exam she asked the proctor to please send her diploma in the mail she was the type of women that was confident in her academics. Before her diploma came in the mail she had already signed up for college to study nursing.

On the outside she looked like she had it all together but on the inside she was empty. She didn't set any standards for her life besides her education. She had been a victim of letting someone else put a price tag on her. She didn't know her worth. She had no idea if she didn't set a standard for her life that someone else will. She was in relationships for all the wrong reasons. She failed to love herself and have a relationship with herself and God. I knew this woman all too well. This woman was me.

I found myself in a toxic relationship because I didn't love myself. To be honest I didn't know how to love myself or where to start. I started to feel worthless.

I felt I was stuck with this person who was overly critical and I was being abused - I was sinking rapidly. Wondering why you feel worthless? You're not alone. It's not uncommon, and usually, it's because someone else has projected these feelings onto you. The problem with feelings of worthlessness is that they can cause bad treatment of yourself, as we often treat things poorly that we don't see as worthy.

Self-worth is how much you value yourself, and it's tied with self-esteem because self-esteem is what we feel about ourselves. If you're not feeling that you have any self-worth, then, simply improving self-esteem isn't enough because you won't believe it inside. You need to improve both to get real results. Many of the same actions improve both self-worth and self-esteem because they're so closely tied together.

Things to Improve on Self-Esteem

We all make mistakes. Concentrating on the big picture too much can make you feel quite small, especially when things don't go right. Instead of striving for perfection and comparing yourself to others, choose to focus on how good you are. Celebrate the things you're good at, even the small accomplishments. Try to avoid looking down at yourself. Instead, talk positively about yourself as if you were talking to someone else. When you talk to others, you often value them above yourself and don't want to upset them. By talking to yourself the same way, you'll be less likely to use thoughts or words that bring you down. Be realistic about things.If you're feeling overwhelmed, lower your expectations a little, and when you've reached a goal, celebrate it. This will mean you're more likely to achieve the goal and might even surpass it.

Build your self esteem

Our Self-esteem is based on how we feel about ourselves as a person. Those with high self-esteem believe that they are adequate, strong, and worthy of a good life, while those with low self-esteem feel inadequate and worthless. Low self-esteem can develop in childhood and continue throughout adulthood, causing great emotional pain. Therefore, it's important to develop a healthy, positive sense of self.

Many people base their self-esteem on external factors, such as how much money they earn, what type of car they drive, and whether people like and appreciate them. If one of these external variables changes, self-esteem can be broadly affected. For example, if your self-esteem is based on the fact that someone else loves you, then you risk feeling extremely vulnerable and worthless if that person's love ends. By the same token, building self-esteem is not an easy task if you have been abused or have suffered years of personal or professional failure.

Building your self-esteem and creating a positive self-awareness comes from taking an inventory of your own strengths and abilities as a human being. Being at peace with who you are and what you have to offer the world is a major part of having high self-esteem. This *inner peace* does not mean that you are unaware of your weaknesses; it merely means that you accept who you are and genuinely like the person you have become.

You should think about yourself as deserving of attention, admiration, and proper maintenance. Avoid the pitfall of paying too much attention to the happiness and well-being of others and too little to yourself. Maintaining self-esteem involves becoming fully aware of your strengths and seeing challenges as opportunities to employ those strengths.

Low self-esteem is often linked to depression or anxiety. If your emotions feel overpowering or out of control, one way to build self-esteem around this issue is to learn to manage your mood and gain control over your feelings. Some people are able to do this with the help of friends and family. Others need to work with a mental health professional to manage the problems that may lie beneath the surface of low self-esteem.

If you struggle with low self-esteem, it is often helpful to connect with others with the same problem. A self-help group, can be helpful in building the skills necessary to believe in your own wishes, needs, and feelings. Self-help groups may be located by talking with a mental health referral service or by asking a therapist or other health professional for a referral. In addition, you can contact your local mental health center about individual and group therapy. Clergy and pastoral counsel may also be of assistance. Other steps you can take to increase self-esteem include looking at community bulletin boards and newspapers for opportunities to demonstrate your skills and abilities, working with others to change the things you don't like about yourself and meditating twice a day to increase your awareness of the current moment and of the goodness of being alive.

Beginning the inner dialogue about who you are and what you have to offer the world is an important process in building self-esteem. However, it is not unusual to have trouble defining your strengths and abilities. Sometimes it is helpful to talk to a therapist about this inner dialogue and about how you might come to the genuine feeling of being a good person who is worthy of the good things in life.

Talking to friends, family, and colleagues can also be useful in further defining who you are and what you have to offer. But, remember that the most important conversation you have about self-esteem is with yourself. Become your own personal cheerleader. Don't be afraid to celebrate even your smallest successes. Ask yourself what you fear, and search within yourself for ways you can cope with these worries and fears. Learning to know and trust yourself is a long but worthwhile process. Throughout life, you may need to search within yourself again and again to find your own empowerment and strength.

Other Actions for Improving Self-Worth

Value is about making yourself feel like you matter or that you make a difference. There are two ways to achieve this: (1) by helping others and (2) by valuing what you already know. Start by making a contribution to your community. Volunteering with people less fortunate than you can show you how much you have to be thankful for. By being thankful, you'll also be able to see what aspects of your day are important. Try to pick five things each day for which you're thankful.

CHAPTER 5:

The Power of The Tongue "Affirmation"

> "We have the power to speak into the universe and declare into the reality the life that we want for ourselves," unknown

*I*t has been said countless times, and I have also found it to be true. There is a whole lot of power in the tongue. It is also a point that is agreed upon by sages across time that the universe is amenable to the energy we give off. Taking together these facts, it is then clear that we have the power to speak into the universe and declare into reality the life that we want for ourselves. I may as well point out at this juncture that this conversely also means that we can engineer into existence our own misfortune. The most potent way of tapping into the energy of the universe and putting to life our thoughts is by affirming into existence what we want.

An affirmation is a statement asserting the existence or the truth of something. It is a way of decreeing into existence a state of life. Just like military decrees, the universe is willing to yield to you if you say it with conviction. The truth is, you are whole, perfect, and complete exactly as you are. When you say an affirmation such as *I am confident and competent*, that statement is true about you and capable of becoming the reality if you are willing to believe it. However, many of us have allowed self - doubt to get the better of us.

Repeating the affirmation over and over will help you erase your self- doubt and imprint the reality of the words you speak into your subconscious until you begin to believe it. The same thing applies to affirming a point about yourself and your existence. By telling yourself that you are confident and competent, you will see yourself begin to behave confidently and competently because your mind will adapt itself to conform to the new belief you express.

The universe has yielded itself to you, and everything you want is available to you. All you have to do is claim it. When the Bible tells us that God gave us the power to multiply and conquer the world, the real translation is that everything has been put into our hands to direct it as we wish. Writing and reciting affirmations is one way of claiming what you want and bringing within your control the agents and principalities of the universe.

The words you drill into your head function as triggers to your subconscious, driving you to act in a manner which will make the mantras you profess ring true. In a similar way, your negative self-talk is reiterated all through your days and has an effect on your life in a detrimental fashion. Implementing very helpful self-talk will certainly accomplish absolutely the opposite.

You don't have to believe your affirmations

When I initially tell people about this, they feel incredulous and stunned. Two questions arise: *Why is it an affirmation if I don't have to believe it? and, Isn't it more like self-deception?* Let me make this a bit clearer. It is great if you do believe your affirmations, but it doesn't matter if you don't. The way this works is quite simple. However, it is important to remember that even falsehoods screamed over time and with much forcefulness begin to sink home as truth, or worst case scenario, possible truth. One may argue that falsehood is falsehood and truth is truth, but in the way our emotions work, the tendency to quickly blur this line is ever present. It is for this reason that history can be rewritten!

The possibility is that when you begin with your affirmations the first time, you may not believe them or at least most of them, especially if your affirmation is a real stretch for you. The key, however, is to just keep repeating and empowering them in spite of the voices in your head telling you that you're lying to yourself. It is really like revving the engine of a bike, it comes to life more with every time you apply pressure.

There is no doubt that this wouldn't be easy, believing a far-fetched affirmation. Think of saying, *I have all the money I can ever want and need,* while you know you only have $748 in your savings account. The natural tendency would be for your mind to focus upon the fact that you're essentially broke. .

When this happens, as it would often happen, try to ignore the negative voices and continue to repeat your affirmations. Know that the voices will be there, and it is perfectly normal. As you continue to repeat your positive affirmations, you will gradually begin to drown out the negative voices, and it will get quieter and quieter. They will probably never go away, but after a while, the voices in support of your affirmations will get stronger, and the negative voices will be in the background, barely audible.

The mind must have repetition in order for it to be convinced and for you to manifest your affirmations into reality. Even when it seems like nothing is happening, keep repeating them. Trust me, it works!

I'll share a true story about one of my affirmations. Would you believe me if I told you that 4 years ago, I did not believe I was capable of accomplishing any of my goals? I didn't believe that I'm beautiful. I would look in the mirror, and see a hurt person. All that stared back at me was a face that was nowhere near amazing; my self-confidence and esteem sunk way down as I reminded myself just how flawed I was. One day I looked in the mirror and took a pair of scissors and started cutting my hair. It was in this state of self-deprecation that I wallowed for a long while. One day, I made up my mind that I was no longer going to continue on this path, the path of emotional, psychological, and even self-abuse. The most important factor in this transition was a realization that I did not need anyone to validate or invalidate who I was. I started empowering and motivating myself by building a strong opinion of myself using affirmation.

I consciously affirmed who I was and my abilities every morning by looking into the mirror and speaking life to myself using what I would describe as the *I am* set of statements. I will share some of these statements with you later on in this chapter.

In the way we have been talking about affirmation, one might be tempted to think that engaging in it is a novel action that requires elaborate planning. The truth, however, remains that affirmations are a very normal way of thinking and that we have been empowering and/or disempowering ourselves with affirmations consciously and subconsciously. To put it succinctly, we have been affirming all our lives, knowingly or unknowingly. Everything you think or say to yourself is an affirmation. In the same vein, anything someone else says to you is an affirmation, if you accept and believe it. Your subconscious mind will adapt and conform to the statement made, whether it is good or bad for you. It is for this purpose that you might want to be more deliberate and strategic with your affirmations.

Who you listen to and keep around you is very important. This is because the more often you keep hearing some statements, the more the tendency that you will start believing them. People don't usually make a conscious decision to program negative motivations into their subconscious mind. It is usually done subconsciously. What is more, even when they realize it, they then tend to rationalize it. For example, if you find yourself saying *I'm broke,* that is an affirmation. You might then find yourself rationalizing it by saying, *I have to be realistic, I am really broke.*

The truth remains that we create our realities. So, if you want that reality, keep saying it and it will come to be. On the other hand, if you would want to change that reality, then you must change the affirmation, and consequently, the belief. That is how you form positive or negative motivations about yourself. By saying these things to yourself over and over (usually subconsciously), these thoughts begin to manifest, and you then have no other option but to accept it as your reality.

You could make it easier for you to attain a complete belief in what you profess by doing the following:

- **Count your successes:** You are a successful person. The truth remains that you are not where you used to be. Progress has been made and I dare say that some of the things you wish you had back then, you now have them. Like every other tendency of man, familiarity breeds contempt. When you attain the new heights you have always wanted and live that reality for sometime, you begin to take it as ordinary. The same things you have now, there are others who still pray and wish they would attain the same feats.

- **Talk to people:** Sometimes we get caught up in our own world getting on with what we need to do, forgetting there is a whole world out there. Go out and meet people – your friends, family or even new people- at a club or activity. This will give you a well-earned break, a new perspective, and you will be able to come back to your work feeling energized and fresh. It will also give you the opportunity of assessing yourself, particularly with good friends telling you about your qualities and abilities. This could go a long way in re-shaping how you see yourself, especially when you have a low perception of what you are able to do.

Why don't you take time off from the problems that seem to be clouding your achievements and really count your blessings and successes one by one? If you do, you will find out that progress has indeed been made. This will give you the confidence you need, that despite the challenges, you have conquered a lot of ground and that you can do more. With this belief that you can achieve new feats and that the weight you attach to things is a function of your own perception, you will start to reassess the situations you face. This will in turn, make it easier for you to build the necessary confidence in yourself, allowing you room to be convinced of the truth of your affirmation. After all, if you have done it before, you can do it again right?

Look back at everything you have achieved to remind yourself how far you have come. Then, use the excitement and energy to plan the next stage – new goals, new projects, and new enthusiasm.

When to use affirmations

- First thing in the morning and last thing before you go to sleep

- While waiting in line or in traffic

- When you feel anxiety, insecurity, or stress

- When you're feeling bad or depressed

- Every time you think about it

How to write affirmations

- Keep them short, simple and easy to remember.

- Always make them positive.

- Keep them in the present tense.

- Never include the words no, not, or don't in an affirmation. Your mind does not recognize those words and it will help you dispense with all the negativities and unwanted energy.

- Include words that will create positive emotions and feelings.

It needs only to be pointed out that it is best to write your own affirmations in the way that suits your particular situation and temperament. However, nothing stops you from using other people's affirmations, as this is one case where the end definitely justifies the means. Here are a few affirmations for success and well-being that you can start with:

- I am a money magnet.

- Money comes to me easily and effortlessly.

- I create my life.

- I create the exact amount of my success.

- I am a genius, and I use my wisdom daily.

- I am powerful and smart.

- I am truly grateful for everything I have right now.

- Lucrative opportunities always come my way.

- I am in perfect health.

- I am a generous giver and an excellent receiver.

- I release and dispense with all subconscious barriers to my success.

- I am calm, confident, and in control.

- I am a calculative goal getter.

- I look and feel great, and I am certainly loved by many!

Know that your thoughts and words are powerful. If you repeat your affirmations every day, coupled with visualizations, you will be amazed at how quickly your dreams will come true. Most importantly, expect to receive your affirmations. Just try it and see for yourself that this really works!

LEADERSHIP IN RELATIONSHIPS

Chapter 6:

---•---

Family is everything

"My 'why' is my family," ~Joi U Grant

Family, where do I start with this one? This is one area that you would agree with me deserves great attention. However, for me, it wasn't until later in life that I realized just how much more I needed to give for my family. Family is very important, and I have always wanted to do something to make them proud. I thought of doing many things, such as joining the police department or going to nursing school. I also thought of going back to school to further my education so that when I retire from the police department, I will have something to fall back on to support my family. I didn't really fancy being a police officer, but it wasn't like I was left with many choices. Making a decision on a career path wasn't really difficult since I had limited choices.

I filled out a nursing school form in the hopes that I could make sure the bills were paid on time and to provide a roof over my daughters' heads. In spite of my plans, unforeseen events occured. These events greatly tested my role as a parent. It was January, and I came down with a cold. Gradually, everyone else in the house also caught the cold. My youngest daughter couldn't seem to shake off the cold. Her fever was very high, and she had a runny nose with a cough that refused to go away. With her temperature increasing, and a continuing complaint of headache, I began to panic. I spent the next six months running from one hospital to another. I ran back and forth from one doctor to another, seeking a diagnosis that would give us some insight into what really was wrong. I was lucky that I had scheduled my vacation within that time so that I could read for my exams. However, the events that followed ensured that the vacation was used for something other than studying.

I still consider myself lucky for the fact that I had half of January off work, which meant I had ample time to take care of my sick child. The diagnoses seemed to change with each new hospital. Doctors suggested everything from viruses, to urinary tract infections, to menstrual issues. The proliferation in diagnoses did not sit right with me, and it got to a point where my daughter was going through a bottle of Motrin daily. I knew this wasn't healthy, and as a parent I felt really bad. I felt I had failed in my duties to my family, and it really broke my heart seeing her suffer like that. The smile was lost from her face, and she lost a lot of weight. Although she wasn't crying, I could see the pain on her face.

So one day, I said to myself, *You have been to every hospital in Brooklyn. You have got to do something else fast.* I talked with my partner about the situation, and he advised that I go back to one of the hospitals where she had already been. I took the advice since there were some medical tests we still needed completed.

We had some more tests run, but five days later, things weren't getting any better. I requested that they do an MRI on her, and after much hesitation, they finally agreed. When the results came out, they found she had an abscess between her frontal lobe. We rushed to yet another hospital for surgery.

Things were happening fast. I really questioned my faith and whether my daughter would make it out alive. It dawned on me that the only thing I had left in life at the moment was prayer. I didn't have time for any second opinion on her condition. Instead of wallowing in self-denial, it was best to just put all my trust in God and call out to Him for help. I knew that if I called on Him, He would be gracious in guiding my steps. As I sat there trying to hold my faith together, the doctor walked in and explained what the procedure was going to be like. She more or less prepped my daughter for what to expect.

It was then that my world really came apart. My two daughters wept. I became really upset, but I was also trying to calm my daughters down. It was a really tense moment. I remember receiving calls from my coworkers. They tried to encourage me; everybody was quite supportive. My supervisor called to let me know that the office would be there for me in case I needed anything.

During most of the calls, I was really incoherent. I wept my heart out. In the midst of all this, I learned that family is not just comprised of one's blood relatives. My coworkers had shown me so much care that I began thinking of *them* as family, immediate family. Sometimes, it takes a situation such as this to realize that anybody can actually be family.

Then came the time for the surgery. The anesthesiologist came to me and requested that I leave the room so that he could prep my daughter for surgery. As I made the walk out the door, I could see the past flash before me. I thought of the many things I didn't say to her, like how I loved her —and the moments when I should have given her hugs. I also thought of how I had not been there for my family during the days spent at work. I remembered the times I was so engrossed with my career that even when I was home, I wasn't really home. I remembered the countless times I chose to do overtime instead of spending quality time with my family. Even when I get home, I would be so tired that I would go straight to sleep. Even though those sacrifices were for them, I realized that the love and quality time could not be purchased by the additional dollars. I felt sad because I realized within that fleeting moment that little kids need quality time with their parents, and that provision does not just mean material things.

So, I was standing there, feeling like I had failed my little girl. When the doctor rushed to administer the anesthetics, I said to myself that this could be the last time I would see my little girl and that those little eyes might close and never open again. In my fears, I was praying to my God, asking Him to give me a second chance with my daughter, a chance to remedy the many failings of my parenting. It was in this most trying moment that I realized the importance of family. The lesson was wide ranging, letting me know the need to spend time and grow with my family as well as the fact that family could be broader than one's blood relatives.

Your colleagues, coworkers, and friends may make up family as well. From that day forward, I made a decision which I kept when she became better. I took out time to hang out with my family. We would go for movie nights, play games together, and have lots of fun. I saw my children grow stronger emotionally, and the bond we shared increased; joy radiated in our lives. I learned the hard way that life, particularly family life, is not all about working to provide material things for your kids. It's also about being available to guide them through a tumultuous life. I set my mind in search of an exit plan that would put an end to my 9 to 5 schedule. I needed a plan that would have a big chunk of the pie chart dedicated to family time, because in the end, they are really all I have.

CHAPTER 7:

How to be in A relationship you deserve

> "If you, as a woman, decide to work on yourself, developing
> your personality, and enhancing your abilities, you would have
> even more value to give and manifold favor to add to whoever is
> the lucky finder," Uknown

*S*ince the time of creation, women have had special purpose. Eve was created by God out of a dire necessity to achieve the completeness of creation. God created woman out of a great need that nature would be grossly inadequate without this pearl of creation.

Pastor John Gray suggests that women are integral parts of life. Life itself takes on greater value and is complete in all its parts with a woman to help you through the journeys that it is.

Whether women realize the blessing they carry and represent as well as the special role they are assigned in creation to pass on favor to their companion. It is in realization of this special gift that it must be added that you don't need to chase after men for your completeness. Some women sometimes feel that they need to hook a man for their own emotional or physical completion, but it only remains to be said that the one who has a lack is the one to seek for solutions for what he lacks. Have you ever seen a rich man begging a pauper to have his money? It is always the other way around. It is in this same way that a woman, who is favor personified, does not go about begging for whom to give it. Rather, the man who needs the help or favor should be the one clamoring for it. You don't need to chase the one that needs the favor. Instead, have the one that needs the favor chase you. You are the one with all the cards. You hold the ace and are the embodiment of value. Whoever you decide to bless with that value is all the better for it!

It wasn't long ago that I realized the truth of this position myself. Since then, it has been a game changer for me. It made me realize who I am and the infinite value I hold within me. It made me realize that I am more than the fears and disenchantments I have about myself, and it certainly gave me a lot of confidence!

It remains to be added that just like gold is sharpened by the flames, even a being of value as yourself can also work to acquire more value. It is like the economy. A strong economy gets stronger with the investments and sound economic policies deployed by its managers. In the same vein, if you as a woman decide to work on yourself, developing your personality and enhancing your abilities, you would have even more value to give and manifold favor to add to whoever is the lucky finder.

We walk around speaking of how we want good men to love us, take care of us, and take care of the household. While this is good and cannot be faulted, the question is: *When the good man finally comes, how prepared are we to nurture the relationship, add value, complement and keep it? Are we ready for the good man?* We can pray for a good husband and a happy home, but while we're waiting, we should work on ourselves.

The other day, I was flying home from Atlanta and the man next to me sparked a conversation, we basically discussed what I have been sharing with you. After listening to him, I had to take a good laugh. Our discussion gave me the opportunity to reflect on all the relationships I have had in the past. I recalled how I went from confusion to chaos, disasters, and failures. I didn't know what exactly I wanted because I hadn't developed myself enough to be able to demand qualities from someone else. I basically drifted along from one person to another, testing the waters as I went. I was going from one bad relationship to the next. I didn't realize I was the favor factor. I dated all types of men: light skinned, dark skinned, tall, slim, educated, uneducated, men with kids or men with no kids. I made excuses for being so rudderless. I recall one encounter I had where I dated a man because he told me that he had a girlfriend, but they didn't have sex. He claimed that she was helping him with his son. At another time, I had a date, and when the bill came, this guy simply put his portion of the bill in the booklet, with no tip or tax included, and winked at me! That was it! I was done with him! I told him he can go kick rocks. In both situations I made excuses for the reason I was treated the way I was.

It was not until later that I realized that all the bumpy rides I was having in my relationships were actually a reflection of the relationship I had with myself. That's right, I said it! The reality, my reality, was a reflection of my inner turmoil, the emptiness and shortage of value I felt inside.

The danger in feeling short of value and not doing anything to shore up yourself is that before long, you might actually take it as who you are. The line between who you are and the qualities you merely need to build up soon blur and you might begin to believe you don't deserve what actually should be yours. You settle for less: abusive relationships, relationships that you are not happy being in, etc. Make sure you do not settle for less than you actually deserve and are worth. As a matter of fact, building yourself up and having a fantastic view of yourself is key to a good relationship with someone else. If you ask me, my advice would be that we don't go about looking for relationships with someone else when our relationships with ourselves and most importantly, God, are weak. The latter relationship is key and gives life to the former.

Having built up yourself, it is then time to ask yourself a few questions and most importantly, provide genuine answers to what you ask. First and foremost, do you know what you want in a relationship? What are your standards from which you will never budge? This, I choose to call the non-negotiable. What other standards can you afford to overlook at first and help your spouse build them up if possible? These are the negotiables. They are things you can try to change, but if they don't work, you would still be happy and fulfilled in your relationship. What are your deal breakers, the things you cannot imagine giving up? Do you have it in you to take little insults in your stride? Can you keep your cool and explain to the other party that you do not appreciate their choice of words used?

Deal breakers may include a man spitting on you, calling you names or labelling you cheap. They may also involve a man making you feel less than you are through verbal, physical, mental, and sexual abuse or plainly showing you that you are not loved. The list is really endless. While the above listed traits are general and would really offend every reasonable person, certain individuals have their own personalized deal breakers which may not hold for the next person. It is then advised that you know your deal breakers.

Most times, when we hear of reasons why people are divorced or incidents that affects them deeply, we might be surprised and think it's just a minor failing. However, the truth is that our deal breakers may be different. That which is an absolute *no* for you might not be the same for me. Other questions you may need to ask yourself are: D*o I think God would sanction this relationship? Did I consult with God about this relationship? Is my partner building me up or tearing me down?*

Above all, know that there is no rush to be in a relationship. I would even add that you establish a relationship with yourself first! Spend time with yourself. Date yourself! Silly right? As silly as it might sound, this is the way to go. The knowledge gained would help you make the right choices and navigate your relationships capably when they happen. After all, who knows better than you what your likes and dislikes are ?

Chapter 8:

———◆———

Self- Leadership

> *As a woman wearing multiple hats you must make it a*
> *priority to become a self leader unknown*

*B*eing the leader of your life and understanding how important it is to recognize and manage your own thoughts, behaviors and emotions is imminent to your success. As a woman wearing multiple hats you must make it a priority to become a self- leader. It requires time, commitment, energy, an open mind and the desire to elevate from where you are to where you want to be. I can tell you from experience, it is difficult to open the pages of your life story and dissect them, but in order to find the leader within it is a mandatory step. Are you ready?

Let me explain what I mean by self-leadership. It is having a developed sense of who you are, what you stand for, what you're capable of achieving and what you want out of life. It also helps to shape your ability to effectively communicate with others, build relationships and influence your behaviors. Self-leadership is a combination of self-awareness, self- honesty, self-knowledge and self- discipline. Understanding that being accountable and responsible for your own thoughts and actions are also critical factors on the path to self-leadership.

Now, let's get into what you need to do to become a self-led, multifaceted, professional woman.

First you must be willing to take the necessary steps to make uncomfortable changes. I was talking to a good girlfriend a few weeks ago and she told me how she had to rediscover herself in order to be the best mother, wife and entrepreneur she could be. She confided in me that her journey to understanding who she truly is, was one of the hardest things she had done in life. She had to take off her masks and confront the woman standing in the mirror and it wasn't pretty for her. She was doing a whole lot of pretending in life. She was pretending to be happy, satisfied in her career and confident and it was causing her to forget who she was and her purpose in life. Her pretending was having a negative impact on her family, her business and her relationships and she knew that she had to make some changes. Changes that would cause her to question herself but ultimately place her on the path to igniting her confidence.

After you take a long, hard look at the woman in the mirror, as she did, and decide to unveil the self-led, confident and highly skilled woman inside, you must discipline yourself. And I don't mean punishing yourself or indulging in self-criticism, I mean discipline your thoughts, actions, reactions, behaviors and habits.

My good girl friend explained that she had to train herself like she trained her three-year-old to use the bathroom. She had to constantly instill positivity into herself which in turn allowed

her to pour positivity into the people and places around her. She said that being the leader of her life allowed her to become a more efficient and committed professional woman that could manage her responsibilities with a lot more ease and comfort. She shared with me that although vulnerability and transparency were challenges for her, the outcome outweighed every doubt and insecurity she had to face.

So, are you ready to take the steps to discover yourself and find the leader within? I want to share 3 easy steps you can take to begin your journey into self-leadership that will help you become a woman with not only a vision but direction.

1. Monitor your self- talk.

2. Be clear on you goals and expectations.

3. Bet on yourself, every time!

Self- leadership isn't just about your career, business, family, personal goals, dreams or desire to be the perfect mother, it is a compilation of all those things and your ability to mix them all together in one bowl and create the most amazing life size cake you've ever seen.

CHAPTER 9:

---❧---

Dealing With Your Naysayers

"If you allow them, your naysayers will deplete you and dismiss your vision. They will kill the ambition in you!"
Unknown

---

*A*t least once in your life, you have probably encountered a naysayer. A naysayer is a person who habitually expresses negative or pessimistic views. Naysayers love to speak their opinion, whether it is valid or not. They say things like, *Why do you want to start that business when you have a good job? You do not have the right credentials or experience to pursue your dream. Think about what might happen if you fail.* They always come around with a negative commentary.

Who are the naysayers? They may be your spouse, parent, sibling, coworker, or a friend. You go to them with your ideas, full of excitement, seeking their support, and before you finish pouring out your heart, they shoot you down. You hope to receive words of encouragement, but instead, you hear words of doubt and fear. If you allow them, your naysayers will deplete you and dismiss your vision. They will kill the ambition in you!

You should try to understand that they probably are not reacting in this way to purposefully discourage you from your dreams. Don't take it personally. For the most part, they are just concerned for you because they do not want to see you get hurt or fail. I also like to call these types of people saboteurs .

There are two types. One will try to sabotage your dreams right from the very beginning because they care too much and want to protect you. The other is the ugliest type that feels threatened and jealous by your dreams of success and happiness because they doubt they can do the same.

Are there any naysayers in your life? Is there someone who is perhaps discouraging you from pursuing your goals and dreams? Is there someone who is keeping you from achieving your highest potential?

I have faced my fair share of naysayers. I grew up in a time where I always worried about what somebody else thought about me or what somebody would say in regards to what I was doing. I always had confusion going on because my focus was on what other people thought of me when I started my career in law enforcement. Moreover, I was embarrassed to tell people what I did because of the negativity about police officers. I thought that would cause them to be biased towards me.

I was ashamed that I was a police officer. It didn't dawn on me until later on, when I had to kill the noise, which means to stop listening to the naysayers. All my life I had been listening to what the naysayers had to say, and that stopped me from advancing in my career as a law-enforcement officer. However, that moment when I decided to stop listening to the naysayers, embrace my own thoughts, and not worry about what they had to say, I became a leader in my life and in my career.

A friend shared his experience with me on naysayers he encountered earlier on in life. He said one of them was his junior college teacher. She would discourage him and his classmates from aiming too high in life. She also pre-judged each student based on her biased assessment of his/her abilities, and then treated the student as such, hence creating a self-fulfilling prophecy. Rather than encouraging them as a teacher, she was often a wet blanket, telling them to opt for pragmatic courses and career paths rather than set big goals and dreams.

When he decided to quit his corporate job in 2008 to pursue his passion, everyone except this particular friend discouraged him. A close friend said he would regret it in the future. Another friend suggested he was crazy. People, personal mentors, and friends alike, advised him against it. Some said that economic recession was coming soon. Others said that his then corporate job was fantastic and that he would never get such a great job in the future. There were also those who said that he was too young and didn't have the right skills and know-how to achieve results in his new path. Some even said that he was wasting his previous education and his career path.

For all the naysayers I faced in the past, I never heeded their words. None of their pre-cautions came true. I went on to achieve every single goal I had set out for and more. It was almost as if they were just projecting their personal fears and

issues onto me. If you are facing naysayers, I want you to know that your life is yours, and you don't need other people telling you what to do. Here are

3 Major Ways To Deal With Naysayers

- *Safeguard your goals from them*

Imagine you're trying to create a beautiful, grand sandcastle at the beach. Now, imagine someone pouring water on top of your castle every minute. Will you be able to build anything in the end? No, of course not. Each time you get anywhere, your creation gets demolished instantly. At most, you'll end up with some clumpy looking lump and a very frustrated you. All the efforts you put in will go to waste. That's the same thing that happens when you listen to the naysayers. Being discouraging and skeptical in nature, they tend to talk about the downsides and horror stories of the dangers surrounding what you plan to do. Every second you spend listening to what they have to say about your goals is just like pouring acid over your dreams. In the end, you have to spend extra time and effort to combat the damage they've done. It's not even worth it, in my opinion.

Whenever you have a burning desire to do something positive in life, it's very hard to not tell everyone you know. You are excited about your vision and you want to tell others. As I have learned, you cannot tell everyone. Your personal vision is too precious to let other people taint it. Protect your vision.

Don't give naysayers the opportunity to damage your vision because they don't see it. Don't let them distract your vision's pursuit because of past mistakes and failures. Protect your vision by minimizing the amount of people you share your life with. Share it with only a few people who you know will encourage you and help you protect your vision. Your goals are too precious to let other people taint them. Protect them. Don't give naysayers the opportunity to damage your dreams. Never raise the topic in the first place.

- ### *Surround Yourself with Enablers*

Negativity tends to play a big role in people's everyday lives. It shouldn't. Then, why does this happen? To be completely honest, it has to do with the set of people you surround yourself with. This is why you need to learn to surround yourself with positive people, because it ends in the result of so much more than you could ever imagine.

The people you surround yourself with have an impact and controlling power over your life. Someone who surrounds themselves with nothing but negative and toxic people, who do nothing but cause pain or put you down, is most certainly not going to live life to the fullest.

Isn't life supposed to be all about happiness and finding the beauty on and within every aspect? For the most part, yes. Of course, there are going to be obstacles and sad times here and there. It isn't going to go your way all of the time. However, one thing you can do to make an impact on your own is to carefully choose the people you surround yourself with. Drop the negative people, and gain the positive souls. Choose the people who reflect you, the ones who have dreams, desires, and ambition.

Choose those who will do nothing but help you push for and realize your own dreams.

I can't even begin to explain how much of an impact this will have on your everyday life. You will go from living each day being put down, to having the feeling of so much you want to change. With a positive mind, that feeling will end up being more of just a thought. It will be followed by a positive reaction with a positive outcome. You will end up being the change that's always been just a thought. You will feel inspired to succeed to the highest and be the greatest you can be.

The power of surrounding yourself with positive people is a power like none other. When you free yourself from negative people, you free yourself to be you, which is truly the only way you should live. You'll learn to love the life you live.

Positive people bring out the best in you, make you happy, and make you laugh. They help you when you're in need, and they genuinely care. They encourage you to go after your dreams and applaud you once you succeed. The power of positive souls in your life makes you become someone who feels good about themselves and their everyday lives. You become inspired. You gain self-respect and confidence. Seems to me, it's time to drop the negativity and gain the positivity, because it has so much more to offer.

Rather than face negativity, surround yourself with positivity instead. You are the average of the five people you spend the most time with, so choose the best five people you want to spend time around. Create Your *Success Network*, the five people you want to emulate in real life.

Think about the people who are supportive or would be supportive of your goals if you told them. Think about how you can increase the time you spend with them starting from today. If you don't have any such people in your life, it's okay. Think of the people out there in this world who are doing what you want to do, then increase your contact with their works, such as their books, their interviews, their TV shows, and so on.

- ***Think Back To Your Vision for Yourself***

Last but not least, think about your ideal vision. What is your ideal vision for your life? I use to think it was a silly waste of time to think about a vision for my life. Who does that? It seems too touchy-feely, too Tony Robbins-ish. But then, as I started learning how to change my life and my habits, I realized something: People avoid creating a vision for their lives because they believe the exercise is futile. Why make a vision when it's impossible to accomplish those things anyway?

I've also noticed something over the past several years. The most interesting, accomplished people I know all have a vision for their lives. They seem to know what comes next, like they've seen the future.

On the other hand, people I meet or know who are stuck and have that hopeless look in their eyes, like they're just passing time in life without joy or aspiration, those people don't have a vision. In fact, many of them don't even have long-term goals. Does having a vision make you better able to change your life, or does being able to change your life make having a vision possible?

Being able to change your life and having a vision for it are the yin and yang of living a great life. They're interdependent and complimentary of one another. One will jump-start the other. Find the motivation to change your life, and you'll be able to create a vision for it or create a vision for life and then learn how to change it.

Whenever you get distracted by naysayers, it's only because you've taken your eyes off your goals. If that's the case, all you need to do is to look back at them. Recall what exactly you want to achieve. Think about what exactly you want to get out of your life. Then, ask yourself if it's worth it to put them on hold because of a couple of naysayers.

Don't deny yourself of the life you should live just because of naysayers. At the same time, make sure you're not being a naysayer to others. While finding the leader in you, don't kill the leader in others through naysaying.

Chapter 10:

⸎

What the Health

"The reason was simple; It was for the food,"
~Joi U. Grant

In my years of battling personal abuse and self-esteem related issues, I realized that personal perception and fitness were the very first steps to determining how I could live with myself and have healthy relationships with others. My battle to get myself in shape and to quit self-destructive diets was one long and dreary challenge. Like everything else in life, my diet had its origin – which over time had become deeply rooted – and it took a conscious effort to let it go. Its origin was traceable to the festive seasons. I can remember looking forward to festive seasons when I was younger –Christmas, Thanksgiving and the New Year. The reason was simple. It was for the food! My grandmother would cook collard greens with ham hock, string beans, black-eyed peas with pig ears, fried chicken, and turkey. There would also be candy yams, macaroni & cheese, and cornbread. I would make lemon cake, strawberry cake, and peach cobbler.

The staple on New Year's Day would be collard greens, which my grandmother, for some strange reason, believed represented money. I remember one year that I had a major headache after eating the black-eyed peas. It was so intense that I dozed off. When I woke up, the headache was gone, and I remember telling my grandma that I thought the pig ears gave me headache. She confirmed my thoughts, telling me that every other person had also complained of a headache. After this, she started taking out the pig ears from the black-eyed peas. This incident made me aware that our diet has a major role and impact on our lives, wellbeing, and appearance. Food has psychological, physical, and emotional implications. Notwithstanding, the fat heavy diet I had growing up, I maintained my figure up til the age of 28. I thought all was fine. However, later indications when I was approaching 30 pointed out to me the need to remain vigilant and pay attention to health, which at the time I wasn't doing. I noticed that everyone in my house was developing one form of chronic illness or another, including diabetes and high blood pressure. Many were developing one form of cancer or another.

I did a little research to better understand my susceptibility to all these; the results further confirmed the need to always pay attention to health. I found that 13.2% of all African-Americans aged 20 years and above have been diagnosed with diabetes while nearly 44% of African-American men and 48% of African-American women have some form of cardiovascular disease. Following my research, I made a decision to make some major changes in my lifestyle. I started with my diet; I overhauled my eating habits.

First, I cut out pork entirely and restricted my consumption of beef. I love to bake, so I still kept my pastries, pies, and cakes in my diet. My resolutions to cut down on baked foods *tomorrow* never came.

Late in my 30's, the effect of the remnants of my unhealthy diet came to haunt me. My bones started to hurt badly, and every time I carried something or tried a little exercise, my joints creaked. I decided it was time to make a change. I became a vegan. My decision to go vegan was influenced by my research which suggested that the pains in my joints could be a result of inflammation. I had to cut out all processed foods and follow a regimented vegan diet. I went *cold turkey*. Then, I began to get creative. I'd have beans for breakfast, lunch, and dinner. Those days were my toughest days, and it was really difficult to stick to my regimen. The fact that this was a new way of eating, coupled with the difficulty of having to find a place that catered for vegan diets, made my decision really hard to stick by. I started meal prepping. It was a great decision on two fronts. First, prepping was a great way for me to save money. Secondly, I could get full on one meal. Now, that meant a lot for me, especially as I was gluttonous at the time, eating six times or more in a single day. After two weeks of strict diet regimentation, my body began to make a recovery. I stopped feeling pains. The results encouraged me to push even further, and I made the next decision to lose weight.

I decided to restrict myself to drinking only warm water with lemon every day. I have been able to stick to this. Coupled with regular exercise, I have been living my best life, health wise. The benefits of becoming vegan are tremendous. Though the process or regimen could be difficult to maintain, you can start small and make gradual substitutes to your diet until you are able to work your way up. I suggest that the best way to start is to substitute one meal of the day with just vegetables.

For water, go for warm water with lemon, the benefits are tremendous; besides aiding hydration, it also supports weight loss and makes for fresher breath. Also, make it a point to go meatless for at least one day and you will immediately feel the difference in your health. Lots of vegetables and less meat will lead to more robust health.

Finally, one of the most important decisions I made was to conduct regular self-examinations on my breasts. Finding out that one of my family members had died of breast cancer made me take this important decision to always check myself. I was afraid of getting scans and yearly mammograms, so I decided to start with self-examinations. I decided to make it a point to examine myself after my monthly periods since this is the time when breasts are less likely to be swollen or tender. For postmenopausal women or women who have had hysterectomies, they should perform the self breast exam on the same day every month. Clinical breast exams such as mammograms are recommended at least once every year for women above the age of 40. For women between the ages of 20 and 39, it is recommended that you examine yourself once every three years. I encourage all women to get physical examinations and pap smear tests regularly.

Chapter 11:

———◆◆◆———

Show Me The money

*F*inances are an important part of life. As a matter of fact, a lot depends on them. They are tied to your personal life, happiness, relationship with others and even mental health. I found this out the hard way when my credit score decreased from 700 to 400 . This was the time when I was in my toxic relationship. My spending habits were ridiculous, and I couldn't stop until I hit my lowest ebbs. I was living from paycheck to paycheck. I owed everybody under the sun, and my creditors were becoming really impatient. My car was repossessed; but before then, I was getting tickets almost every day that my car was being towed. My affairs were in shambles. It dawned on me that I had to do something really fast to change the tide of my life

I started becoming creative with ways to make money. I decided to start coaching classes aimed at helping people with personal development To me, this was an exit plan. But then, it dawned on me that I needed to get my own personal development together first! I mean, here was someone who was falling apart talking about helping people with personal development. It was like giving out what you do not have. So, I concluded that the best place to start was with my finances. I decided to start living on a budget; but, first I had to clear my debts to be free and know how much I was worth.

I started by calling up my numerous creditors to find out how much I owed; I had lost count of it all. I was scared and ashamed at first, but then I decided to swallow my pride and put on my big girl panties to start making the calls. I made plans to pay them all.

To learn how to put a cap on my spending, I joined the *Live Richer Academy* to learn the first steps to financial prudence. At the academy, they teach you how to make a budget and the keys to sticking to your budget. I took stock of my expenses, including the money that I spent eating out for lunch everyday with my friends. I also considered the cost of my utilities, my car, and my car insurance. Next, I began to evaluate my credit cards in order of their interest rates. I called up to find out what the interest rate was on each card, and I decided to pay down on my credit cards based upon the interest rates. I paid the cards with the highest interest rates first. When I was done with the credit cards which had the highest interest rates, I worked my way down to the others until I was able to pay everything. To date, I still keep those credit cards, preferring not to cut them up, as a reminder of the successful struggles I put in to get my life together.

Having cleared out my debt stables, the next thing I did was to look at what expenses I could cut out. I thought of my cable bills. *How could I save some money on this?* I called up the cable company, enquiring if they had any promotions running that I could sign up to get my bills lowered. Next, I had to cut down on my cell phone bills. I called the company and asked if there were any promotions that might be of help? It was really difficult sticking to my new austere budget. To keep things in shape, I thought of making my own meals instead of eating out every week. To help me with this, I put myself on a bi-weekly budget of how much I could spend eating out.

The above chronicles my journey and efforts as I set goals for almost everything and in all aspects of my life. I realized that I didn't have any financial goals before then. Once I was debt free, I was fine; but that wasn't enough financial responsibility. I needed to keep tabs on my finances, set a yardstick to measure my capital inflow and outflow; so I drew a plan which I called my *Show Me the Money Plan.*

Through this plan, I was able to follow the trail of where my money went. I listed all my expenses and began keeping receipts of all purchases made. I kept a box where I kept every receipt of purchases made, whether big or small. If I bought a laundry detergent or a snack, I asked for a receipt. Before then, I was in the habit of never asking for a receipt to anything. With the clear picture I got from this money trailing, I was better positioned to address my finances. I went for even more tightening of expenses, and this time, the next port of call was my ATM withdrawal charges. The ATM usually charges $3.50 for each withdrawal. I

devised a way to cut down on the expenses incurred from withdrawals. I would withdraw all the money I would need for a while at one time to cut down on the withdrawal charges.

Next, was to plan for my transportation. Since I no longer had a car, I had to plan for alternative means of transportation; so, I laid out the planned expenses on Uber rides. With this greater responsibility with my finances came a growth and a better management of my affairs. I was not wealthy still, but again I was not broke, at least not as broke as I used to be. I have thus always encouraged everyone I come across to adopt the *Show Me the Money Plan.* You could tailor yours after mine or you could plan a totally different financial regimen for yourself. The most important thing is to stick to whatever you have come up with. It might seem very difficult to be financially responsible, especially as unforeseen contingencies might pop up once in a while; however, sticking to your plan is surely a rewarding exercise. Take charge of your finances, and you will soon see how every other piece of the puzzle would fall in place.

CHAPTER 12:

———— ✤ ————

Self-Care Tips for Busy Women

> *"To give your 100% to everyone while forgetting yourself is mentally and physically draining," Unknown*

For many women, the busy cycle hardly ever ends. Before one day comes to an end, the challenges that need to be tackled the next day are already presenting themselves. It's easy to get caught in an endless web of activities at home, at work, and other social or religious organizations. As a law enforcement officer that's in charge of training new recruits, a mother of two adorable girls, and a caregiver to my grandfather, I think I know a thing or two about losing yourself in the service of others. Your work and family demand nothing short of your *A-game,* and you naturally would want them to have the best of you. In the process of trying to please them, it is quite easy to forget to take care of yourself.

Trying to give 100% to everyone while forgetting yourself is mentally and physically draining. You can only live this kind of life for so long before it starts taking a toll on you. Moreover, you shouldn't wait until then before accepting that you need to take

better care of yourself. You can only perform all the multiple roles expected of you if you remain healthy. However, just how can you maintain your mental and physical well-being with the seemingly endless pressures from everywhere? I'd love to share some self-care tips that worked for me. I believe they would work for any woman struggling to strike a balance between external demands and personal care.

- **Have a self-care schedule:** You cannot rely on spontaneity if you want to get serious about self-care. Waiting until you have the time is never an ideal plan because the time would never be available. The best thing you can do for yourself is to forcibly create time out of your busy schedule. For me, I take a day off to destress and rid myself of any mental clogs. Lifestyle expert, Rebecca Cafiero, also affirmed this in her TEDx talk. If you do not have a self-care schedule, you are not serious about it. If you cannot afford a whole day, a morning or afternoon could prove adequate as long as you are sure you can avoid all forms of external disturbance.

- **Meditate:** We tend to ignore the importance of meditation as a spiritual exercise. In addition, if you think meditation is only for religious or mystical people, you couldn't be more wrong. Meditation connects your body with your soul and helps you find peace from within. As you become more familiar with meditation, you'll find out it's easier to shut out external thoughts during your meditation routine. It helps you clear your head and shut out disturbing thoughts. Personally, meditation is a major

part of my morning routine as it sets me up for a great day. On my self-care day, I have the luxury of spending more time meditating.

- **Never forget the things that make you happy:** Okay, I know things can never be the same with kids and other responsibilities. However, you will enjoy your life more if you do not lose touch with the things that make you happy. You can draw a list of those things and fix it in your timetable, even if it is only once a week. You can choose to volunteer at the soup kitchen, people watch at the park, or go to the cinema with a friend. Just choose anything that doesn't seem like work to you and gives you a sense of fulfillment. We all need to engage in such activities more frequently.

- **Keep a journal:** A journal keeps you from worrying about the fact that time is moving fast. If you find yourself constantly worrying about how quickly the time is going, you are only disturbing yourself with just another thing you have no control over. Keeping a journal helps you to worry less since you actually have a record of what you have done with your time. I write in my journal every night, and I see that time as an opportunity to reflect on what I achieved that day. Personally, I prefer to dwell on the positives and leave out the negatives. I know the last thing I want to see if I happen to read my journal 20-years-later is that an angry waitress spoke to me rudely on a particular day. I also pen my worries in the journal

because writing them down makes my heart less heavy. You can inculcate that habit too; it helps!

- **Pay attention to your body:** A common trend among busy women is that they ignore their bodies. Your self-image depends greatly on how you look. Even if you are too busy to care today, believe me when I tell you that you may end up regretting the neglect when tomorrow comes. Go for that facial, go to that spa, register at that gym, schedule that massage session; just do anything that would help you glow and keep you in shape. Although you may not have the time for elaborate beauty or exercise routines, there are many simple ones that would still do a good job.

- **Sleep well:** You'll be sacrificing a lot if you want to perform well as a mother, worker, caregiver, and the many other roles the society expects you to fill. However, your sleep is one thing you should never sacrifice for anything. Nature, as they say, cannot be cheated. Do not think you have some superhuman ability if you find yourself sleeping much less than you should. Instead, you should work on how you can have more restful nights. Director of the Sleep Disorders Center at the University of California, Alon Y. Avidan, shares this sentiment. He drove home the fact that sleep deprivation could have dire consequences. Moreover, adults should endeavor to sleep for at least 6 hours every day.

I made a deliberate decision to prioritize self-care because I know there is no way I can radiate happiness in my home or at work if I am dying inside. The last thing I want for my family or colleagues is to experience a mechanical me. I wish to live my life fully at any point in time and I only started doing that when I decided to take care of myself.

Prioritizing Your Leadership

Chapter 13:

Goal Setting And Goal Mapping

> "WE ALL HAVE DREAMS, POINTS WE AS-
> PIRE TO BE IN LIFE, AND THINGS WE HOPE
> TO ACHIEVE,"

---

*G*oal setting and mind mapping are two important aspects that go hand-in-hand in finding the leader within. We all have dreams, points we aspire to be in life, and things we hope to achieve. Think about how you plan your trip when going on a vacation. You make arrangements for the hotel, flight tickets, tourist attractions, and most likely, you map out how you'll get to these spots. In this simple analogy, your vacation is your dream and all the planning and mapping out you do before going are your goals. You'll agree you are unlikely to enjoy your vacation if you do not plan ahead.

This analogy can be applied to our lives as a whole. If you aspire to have a happy and fulfilled future but refuse to set clear goals on how to get there, you are leaving that future to chance. Perhaps things would work out just fine or perhaps they may not. Goal setting is how you take control of your future and ensure that you do not just live haphazardly. Planning adequately and working hard towards achieving that plan greatly increases your chances of living your dream. The same applies with organizations and business plans. An organization would have goals that are clearly stated in their vision and mission statement. The route to achieving those goals would be elucidated in their business plan. The importance of goal-setting in living a happy and ful-filled life cannot be overemphasized.

When do you need to set goals?

When many people hear about goal setting, they feel it's an ac-tivity they should leave for their biggest or ultimate dreams only. It's easy to forget that it is the small victories that we are able to record that spur us to achieve more. Goal setting can be applied to every aspect of your life as long as you have something you are working towards. That which you are working towards is, in fact, the goal. Goal setting as an activity only makes you more conscious of it. Below are some aspects of your life where you may apply goal setting.

- Finance

- Personal development

- Family and Relationships

- Health, etc.

Your health goal, for example, may be to eat healthier or to quit smoking. Once you consciously set goals, you make them a part of you. Thus, you tend to push yourself until you achieve the goals.

How to Set Goals and Achieve Them

The following are some tips that can help you with goal setting and ultimately achieving your goals:

Think big

You might consider this advice rather queer since all the goal-setting advocates you've come across probably advised you to set realistic goals. But come to think of it, is there any real achievement in attaining a goal we can easily conceive? What then is the purpose of goal setting when it cannot propel us to achieve what we thought was impossible? When setting goals, you should never cage your mind in the illusion of impossibilities. You should always let your mind wander freely and imagine yourself achieving the inconceivable.

The greatest inventors and those that have become household names today didn't reach their achievements by dreaming and playing small. The Wright brothers were able to invent and fly the first airplane because they imagined without inhibitions. You should emulate this trait while setting your own goals. The saying shoot for the moon, even if you don't hit the mark, you'll land among the stars becomes applicable here. When you set big goals, you'll achieve big things even when it appears you did not meet your goals.

Imbibe the art of reverse engineering

When your goals scare you, it is only normal to find it hard to map out a clear path towards reaching them. But, this slight problem shouldn't be enough to deter you. The technique of reverse engineering would help you greatly here. Imagine your future self, basking in the euphoria of all the goals you have been able to achieve. Now, think back and replay how you were able to achieve those goals. Make a mental note of the obstacles you faced, the catalysts to the goals, and the possible character flaws that almost let you down. If your image of the future is vivid and compelling enough, you shouldn't have any problem figuring out these details. Although things may turn out differently, the compelling image you have about the future should drive you on.

Starve your distractions

The greatest obstacle you will face in the quest to achieve your goals will most likely come from within. At the end of the day, it will all come down to how well you are able to feed your focus and starve your distractions. Once you have your goals clearly mapped out, it should be much easier to overcome the distractions. Anytime you are about to make a decision, you should ask yourself, *Does this take me any closer to my goals or draw me away from them.* Your answer should determine if you'll follow through with the decision or not.

Give yourself a deadline

An open-ended goal is never easy to achieve. You might easily fall victim to procrastination until you eventually discover that it may just be too late. But, when you make your goals close-ended, you might work actively towards achieving them within the timeframe you have set for yourself. So, set a time limit for your goals. Make sure to do that today because by postponing it until tomorrow, you will only be losing more time.

Want your goals badly enough

Ask yourself, *what would happen if I don't achieve my goals?* If the answer you get is an attitude of nonchalance, one that tells you, *life goes on, no matter what,* then you probably do not want your goal badly enough. When you desire something with all your heart, you can't get comfortable with the thought of not achieving it. The case should be the same for your goals. Want them so badly that the thought of not achieving them makes you cringe. It is this drive that could motivate you during the moments you think about giving up.

Using mind mapping to track your goals

When you set goals, it is important to write them down. For one thing, writing your goals down makes them more lucid. You also avail yourself of the opportunity of revisiting the goals when your mind drifts away from them. But, writing the goals down cannot be as effective as writing them on your mind. The technique of imprinting your goals on your mind is known as **mind mapping**.

The technique was first described by Tony Buzan; he identified three elements your goals must have before you can mind-map effectively. Your goals must be:

- Structured

- Memorable

- Visual

Mind mapping can help you bring your goals alive in a way you never thought possible. It involves using a one-page chart to represent your thoughts and pasting it where you can take a look at it anytime. Since all the elements of the goal are on a single page, you can easily measure your progress and assess the work ahead. As you become more familiar with the chart, it becomes fixed in your mind.

Goal setting and mind mapping have worked for me over the years, and that's one of the reasons why I'm very passionate about them. I learned the techniques at a point in my life when I was trying hard to figure out if the path I took was the right one for me. Nursing school was proving to be too much more of a challenge than I anticipated. Coping with academics and other extra-curricular activities soon became a nightmare, and I found myself drifting into an abyss where I didn't want to be. Goal setting and mind mapping helped me out! I had to clearly define my goals for nursing school and chart out ways to achieve them.

I kept staring at the chart every day until the mental picture was stamped on my mind. This helped me pursue my goals with a new fervor and drive. Ultimately, I came out of nursing school with my head held high. Ever since, I've applied the goal setting and mind mapping techniques to every aspect of my life, and I have been reaping the rewards.

CHAPTER 14:

─────❖─────

Being Organized

> *"You are more productive when you're focused and organized,"*
> ~Joi u Grant

I think we can all agree that chaos breeds unhappiness. Whenever you're feeling disorganized, out of control, buried under clutter, or in total disarray, life just feels heavier.

Now, it may seem like some people have been born with an *organizational gene*. They effortlessly manage everything and anything with ease. And, they always have a clean home (of course). But even if you weren't born with the ability to organize, you can learn this valuable skill. And, it may make you much happier in the long run. Like anything that grows and thrives, all that's needed is a little bit of patience, commitment, and love (self-love). Want to learn how to be happier? Let's take a look at the benefits of being organized and the kind of joy it can bring into your life.

Why should You be well organized?

- *It can help you to destress*: Coming home from a long day at work to face piles of clutter, or a lengthy to-do-list, seems like the perfect recipe for more stress and anxiety in your life. But, did you know that there have been actual scientific studies on this phenomena? It's been discovered that people who live in cluttered homes, or environments full of unfinished projects, are more likely to experience fatigue, depression, and higher cortisol levels, compared to those who described their clean home space as restful and restorative.

- *It Boosts Your Productivity:* Quite simply, organization boosts productivity because there is less distraction – whether that distraction is a cluttered desk, a cluttered inbox, or a cluttered schedule. When you're organized at work, you'll be more efficient and likely to get done earlier. When you're organized at home, it means you can focus on getting proactive with your fitness goals, or immerse yourself in healthy cooking. So, if you're someone who thinks all that multitasking is saving you time (i.e. you'll be able to kill five birds with one stone) it is, in fact, slashing your productivity and efficiency.

- *You'll get to snooze better:* One of the things that keeps people awake at night is incessant fretting over everything they have to get done. A chaotic day can also lead to staying up to all hours, just trying to get through everything. Even worse, you may bring your computer into bed while finishing up. Staying up late with an agitated headspace will not help you to sleep. Organization, however, can help you to destress and keep that anxiety at bay, by keeping a decent bedtime and keeping your bedroom a serene place for resting. Another chaotic habit that might impact your sleep is bedroom clutter. If mess equals stress, and stress equals insomnia, then you can see the problem. Your bedroom should be used as a sanctuary for rest and relaxation. Keep it tidy. You should also make your bed every single day, not because your mother said so, but because making your bed in the morning starts your day off productively!

- *It Can Cure your eating habit:* You probably know someone – or maybe that someone is you – whose life got turbulent, and they started to pack on the pounds. It's not at all unusual. A chaotic life leads to chaotic eating. You start by snacking on sugary foods and drinks, desperate for an extra energy boost. You grab-and-go from unhealthy takeout stores. You prepare pre-packaged, additive-drenched meals for dinner. And you've most definitely stopped exercising because there just isn't any time. One of the greatest barriers to healthy habits is A lack of time. But, you can claim that time back by getting organized. When you're organized, you'll be able to find pockets of time to plan meals, grocery shop, and prep healthy, nutritious choices for the day ahead. Some organized people even do a big cook-up on the weekend to get them through a week's worth of healthy meals. That's a pretty smart idea.

- *It helps Goal-setting:* Following through on those goals is one of the keys to an organized, happy life. Goal-setting teaches you to plan, to implement, and to record any progress – whether it's a big event, or just your grocery shopping for the week. Goal-setting can also help to ensure that a regular exercise routine doesn't go out the window with your crazy schedule. It does take more than will power to keep those workouts on the schedule.

- ***Orgenized Time***: The benefits of being organized far outweigh any perceived notion that you're not the *organized type*. And, organization need not be something to dread. In fact, you may even learn to love the stress relief it provides. It also becomes much easier when you don't let things build up to a point of total disarray. If you want to know how to destress and be happier in a seemingly crazy world, then start by being the authority. Put your clothes in the hamper, keep workspaces clear of clutter, teach your kids to pick up after themselves, wash dishes right after you eat, and find a scheduling tool (on your computer, or a written diary) and use it to actively schedule your time.

CHAPTER 15:

It's All in Your Morning Routine

"When you start your morning on the right note, your day automatically becomes more productive,"

~ Joi U Grant

To find the leader in you, you must inculcate some habits. Having a morning routine is one of them. For a long time in my adult life, mornings were my least favorite time of the day. I'd struggle to get out of bed every day, giving myself just about 20 minutes to prepare for work. A quarter of the already short time would be spent looking through my news feed on Facebook and Instagram. Then, I'd find myself rushing to get the kids up and get us all out of the house so I could make it to work just in time. As you can guess, my bed and virtually every other part of the home would be left in a huge mess.

I'd find myself struggling to fully settle down at work. Often, the day would breeze past, leaving me always trying to catch up. After the close of work, I'd rush again to pick up the kids, help them with their homework, and cook dinner; I'd do all this while trying to sort some of the mess I'd left in the morning. I would convince myself that this self-repeating cycle was only hard to stop because I'm not a morning person. However, I did not need anyone to tell me that my life, as it was, wasn't productive. I had no time to study or research more about my business, and I always found myself wishing there were more than 24 hours in a day.

I knew something had to be done if I truly wished to attain any reasonable level of success. I stumbled on an article online that focused on the importance of having a morning routine and how it is germane to productivity and success. Alas! I realized an inability to use my mornings productively was the root of my problems. We all want to be successful, but only a few are willing to pay the price. Below are two important reasons why you should have a morning routine:

- *It increases your productivity*

When you start your morning on the right note, your day automatically becomes more productive. You give yourself that much-needed head start that puts you ahead of your daily tasks. You have enough time and consciousness to prepare and plan for the day. Conversely, if you wake up in a rush, you'll find yourself playing catch-up all day long.

- *It gives you more time to yourself*

Ideally, the morning should be your alone time. It's the only time when you're uninterrupted from the outside world. As you go through the day, challenges pop up from every corner, and you can't help focusing upon them. The morning gives you a chance to plan what you want to reflect upon from the previous day, if need be, and to plan what you want to achieve for the new day.

When you start your day with a morning routine, you invest in yourself first. You reap the dividends of this investment throughout the day. A good morning sets the tone for a good day and a good life is simply a collection of many good days. Here are 11 morning rituals that helped me add momentum and success to my day.

1. **Wake up before everyone else**: The few hours before sunrise are the best hours you have to plan out your day. If you want to do this effectively, the last thing you need is the distraction from your kids or partner. So, ensure you wake up long before they do.

2. **Thank God for that for which you are grateful**: This is the shortest path to achieving your goals. If you don't take time out to appreciate the things you have, you won't get the things you want. No matter how dire you think your situation is, remind yourself that this current life was all you ever dreamed of some years back. Remind yourself that you're living the dream of many others. So, keep pushing on while appreciating the seemingly little things.

3. **Drink a glass of lemon water:** Your body loses a lot of water while sleeping, and you typically go several hours without as much as a sip. Drinking water first thing in the morning jump-starts your system, setting vital organs in motion.

4. **Brush your teeth with the opposite hand:** When you do this, you're activating a hemisphere of your brain you don't normally use. You are thereby releasing more neurotransmitters in the brain. This ultimately leads to more brainpower and a more heightened brain function.

5. **Pray for 10 minutes:** Praying every day bestows spiritual strength. What better time to do this than first thing in the morning?

6. **Read for 10 minutes:** We all know that reading is critical towards attaining success in life. Get something to read at the beginning of your day. Read something motivational or spiritually uplifting would do.

7. **Write down your goals for the day:** This is the point where you plan your day. Writing down your goals gives you a clear idea of what you want to achieve for that day. It allows you to focus upon the important tasks and steer clear of distractions.

8. **Make up your bed:** You'll start your day with a clean environment, and you'll come home to meet a clean environment. Making your bed early in the morning gives you a sense of achievement and a power to conquer. Since you have achieved something positive that day, there's nothing that can stop you from achieving greater feats.

9. **Listen to a motivational audio or video:** What we take in influences our thoughts. A motivational speech inspires you to go about your day with the mindset of

an achiever. It puts you in the right spirits, and ultimately increases your self-belief.

10. **Exercise:** While I'm brushing my teeth, I do leg raises and calf raises. Though I'm still working towards it, I'm not at the point where I can do a full workout . It's great if you can. I also need to emphasize the importance of exercise to your health and well-being.

11. **Make Affirmations:** While I'm touching up my hair, I'm looking into the mirror and reciting my affirmations on the goals I made and about myself. This puts me in the right frame of mind to breeze through my day with confidence.

Since I adopted this morning routine, my life has changed drastically. I'm better focused on achieving my goals, and I have more time to myself. I attain levels of productivity I was only able to aspire to previously. Right now, 24 hours does not seem like such a short time. If you can adopt this morning ritual, it will be great. If you could come up with another one that works for you, it's all good still. Remember, our lives are only a sum of many days. So, if you are able to get your days right, you'll definitely become a good leader.

CHAPTER 16:

❧

Mentorship

"If I have seen further than others, it is by standing on the shoulders of giants,"
Isaac Newton

---

*I*n order to discover the leader in you, the need for mentorship cannot be overemphasized. Benjamin Franklin said, "Tell me, and I forget, teach me, and I may remember, involve me, and I learn." It doesn't matter what line of work you're in, we all need someone in our corner who is going to cheer us on and give us a kick up the bum when necessary.

I'm not referring to a critical parent or a bossy friend who thinks they've got it all together and revels in your misfortune or missed steps. No one needs that, and if you have it, you need to learn to silence those voices in your lives. What I'm referring to is much deeper and more than someone pointing out your foibles. I'm referring to a mentor, someone who **sees** you and sees what you're capable of and who you really, truly are. A mentor is someone who listens and helps guide you along the path, not in an *all the answers* type of way, but in a leading question kind of way. They walk alongside you, listen, and ask smart and healthy questions that cause you to come to conclusions on your own.

A mentor isn't someone who marks your test score; preferably, they are someone who helps you come up with your test questions. They help guide you and keep you on course. A mentor is often older and more seasoned in an area of life that you have identified as successful by your measurement tool.

Perhaps you have watched them with their children who are older than yours. Maybe it's the way they manage their finances or negotiate relationships with teens or how they build into their marriage. Maybe it's business related, and they have developed a strong business with a great company culture. It could be their physical being, the way they care for themselves. It could also be their spiritual walk and the way they just seem to keep it together. They may radiate peace and satisfaction with all facets of life. It doesn't matter what it is, what matters is that you've seen something you admire in the way they conduct themselves and live their lives, and you are curious as to what their influence in your life would be .

I want to encourage you. Whatever stage of life you're in, put up your hand. Let people know that you are keen to have a mentor speak into your life. Be brave and tuck yourself under someone who has gone before you, who has blazed trails and has broken through glass ceilings. I promise, as you do this, your life will only be enhanced for good. Remember, this isn't a *tsk tsk* kind of relationship whereby you are always being criticized and rebuked. Instead, this is a relationship built on mutual trust and respect.

What To Watch Out For In a Mentor?

In the words of Sir Isaac Newton, mentors extend vision and enable proteges to attain greater heights. In short, mentors provide undeniable counsel and resources that are not readily available. One of the key realities on our journey is the fact that you will discover that you cannot *do, go* or *be* all you can be, all by yourself. You will eventually need people, and people will need you. Invariably, you will discover that no one is an island. Our interconnections are obvious realities that remind me of the popular adage on vacuums. It is true that no one can exist or succeed in a vacuum. Each one of us will require other people's help, support, insight, feedback, and resources at one point on our journey.

Coincidentally, the value of mentoring goes beyond oneself. It is a gift that keeps on giving. I am reminded of this scripture, Proverbs 11:14, that says, "In the multitude of counselors (mentoring) there is safety." I truly believe that. I'm sure you do too, no matter your religion. Great mentors provide intangible resources and vital tools not otherwise available or accessible. Mentees benefit from the experience, access, and vantage point of mentors. In my humble opinion, great mentors are the proverbial *wind beneath one's wings.*

Here are some undeniable attributes of great mentors:

- Great mentors show interest in your success.
- Great mentors are vested in your success.
- Great mentors are aligned with your best interest.

- Great mentors focus on helping you be the best you can be.

- Great mentors do not compete with you but rather compliment you.

- Great mentors are not afraid of your successes or threatened by them.

What Mentors Do?

- **Mentors Coach:** Mentors coach and prepare you for change. The economy of the new workforce does not operate solely on hard work but rather on smart work. You need to get smarter about people, relationships, processes, opportunities, and strategies. Great mentors help you get smarter with their wise counsel. I led and organized a youth group for more than eight years with the aim of unearthing the goldmine in these young folks walking aimlessly in life. I coached them cooperatively and one on one. Many of them took interest in joining the academy, and it has helped them in having a grip over their career choices.

- **Mentors Motivate:** Mentors fine tune and transform your vision. They provide ideas, thoughts, and insights that challenge and enable you to see beyond your sphere of influence. Mentors amplify visions by elevating your thinking capabilities. Mentors elevate you by making their shoulders your platform. They prop you up. This demonstration of trust must not be abused as their extensions are critical validations that will eventually open doors and grant you access to opportunities beyond your circle.

- **Mentors Challenge:** Mentors push you to go farther. They refuse to let you settle on your oars and invariably challenge you to go farther than you can possibly imagine. They pat you on the back for your successes, guide you in extracting lessons from your failures, and push you far.

- **Mentors Protect:** Mentors protect you from missteps. Mentors protect and nurture their proteges from premature exposure. They provide insights on how to navigate political landmines in organizations and how to make sound business decisions in your startup or engagements. Their counsel prevents missteps that could otherwise derail your success. Mentors, by their sound counsel, guide proteges from ending up in pits. Their services are almost free. Unlike a life coach or a business coach, mentors don't have an hourly rate attached to them. Usually, they have agreed to a mentoring experience/encounter with you because they genuinely like you and see great things in and through you that they want to invest in. A mentor is different from a life coach in many ways. In many cases, some people I know have both. Free doesn't mean casual. A good mentor will set times to see you and will stick to the time they have for that meeting. It may feel much like a meeting only because there needs to be some structure to your connecting also, they will hold you to a plan and will help you determine

- **Mentors Advise:** Mentors share life lessons. Mentors use their stories and perspectives to paint pictures of what is possible. They use words and their actions to support you. Invariably, they build you up for more than you ever thought possible. Lastly, mentors never give up on you. They never quit believing, encouraging, and engaging their protege. Great mentors assume the vision of their proteges until it is a reality.

I remember when I was completely ignorant of all of these benefits of mentorship. My life was in a mess. I didn't have a shoulder to lean on career wise, and I missed the needed boost that comes from having a mentor. I tell you today, you cannot make a remarkable impact in life without the needed boost of mentors.

So friends, I encourage you to find someone who can speak into your life in this way. If you've identified someone you admire or would love more of in your life, then put up your hand. Let them know you're keen and willing. If they are open to it, let them know you would like to explore what a mentoring relationship could look like. Remember, they are probably new at it so there could be a few bumps in the road. Hold tightly to the arrangement and let it flow as it should.

some outcomes and strategies to get you from where you are, to where you want to be.

Conclusion

Thank you for reading this book. I hope it has been motivating and encouraging. I would like you to learn from all my experiences and use them to build the leader in you. You're wonderful, and you have the power and energy to reach greater heights!